The False Romance

Piyush Nayyer

NOTION PRESS

Published by Notion Press 2024

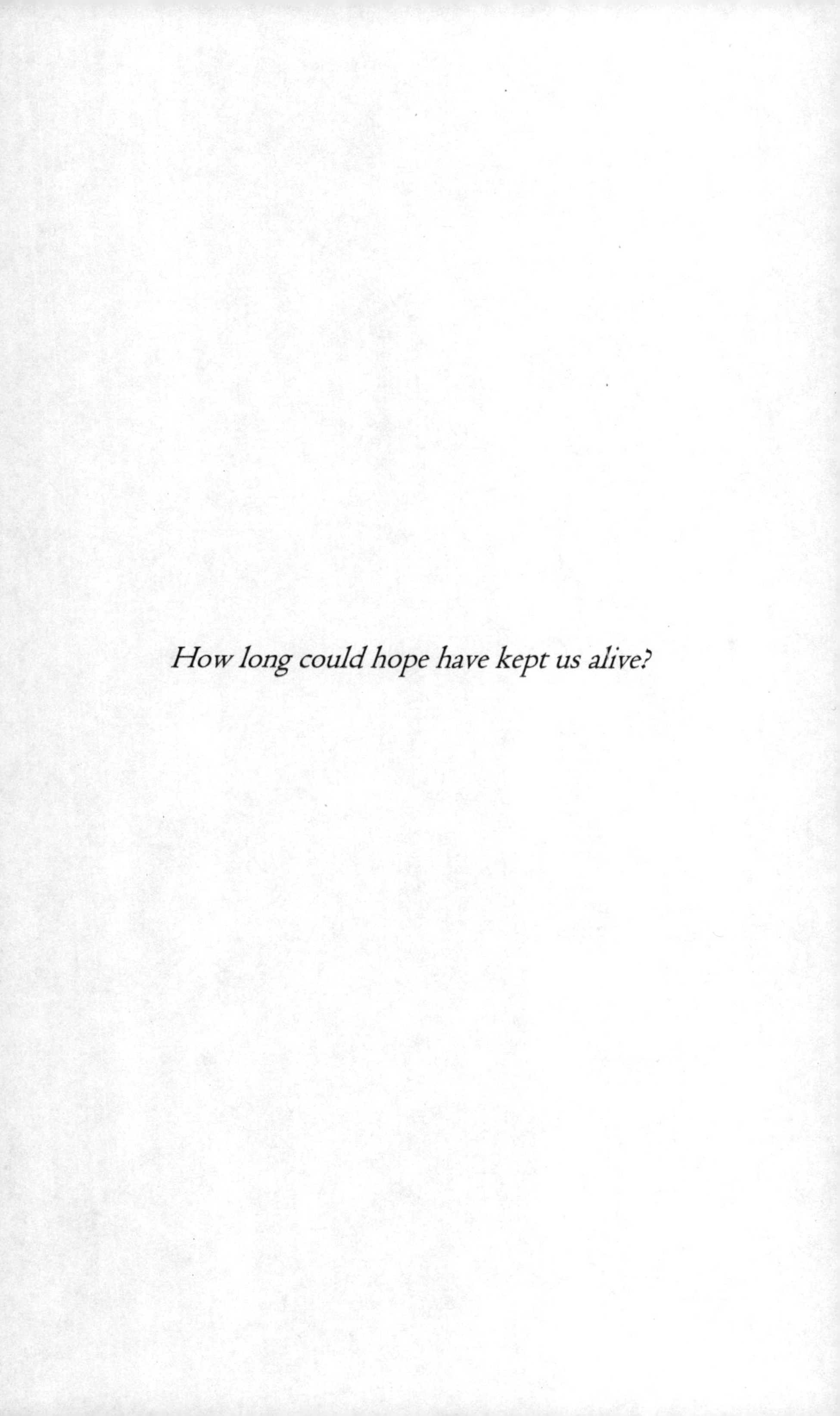

How long could hope have kept us alive?

Table of Contents

Mine

But this time
I'm feeling fine
I think
I'm past all my crimes
I'm dreaming of you tonight
Can you please just be mine?

Fairytale

I think I've been thinking too much
Thinking too much about you and me
I've been very fond of you
Fond of you like I've never been

All the sweet talks on the call
And the love bombs
You keep dropping on me
I've been feeling like
I'm in a fairytale
Living dreams of true love

I think I've been thinking too much
Thinking too much if you could be
You could be my forever love
But I'm not sure if you'd agree

All the chills I get when you touch me
I like it when you look at me
You stare right straight into my soul
I'm so invested in you, baby

But please don't change
I'm too soft to get hurt
I think if this would ever end
It would destroy my whole world
But I'm still gonna risk it
For my fairytale dreams

Whatever happens, happens

I’m So Fucking Stupid

My friend told me I made it worse for her
The person I'm seeing says I think too much

The voices in my head keeps telling me some shit
Drag me down to hell
I’m so fucking stupid

I look in the mirror
Stare and try to fake a smile
My own reflection shows me
My insecurities I try to hide

Everyday's a battle
Of surviving the worst
In the night I search for something
Of comfort and some trust

But I keep feeling
Alone all the damn time

Cheering myself up
But slowly I'm losing my shine

Everything is changing
I can’t catch it up
The world is moving fast
I feel like I’m stuck

Push me to the finish line
I’m lacking behind
I don’t wanna miss out on anything
Of this world which is so divine

'Honey'

Call me 'honey'
Make me your babe
I won't let anybody
Come in our way

I've been watching you for quite some time
Deeply noticing your pretty smile

You light up my day
When I think of you
How good it would be
If I were there with you?

Tell me your secrets
Share me your stories
I wanna know you
And vanish all your worries

You put me on cloud nine
I forget about everything
Living in the daydreams
Of what our reality could be

So call me 'honey'
Make me your babe
I won't let anybody
Come in our way

Is Life Fair?

I never understood a thing about
High fun
Chill vibes
Floating away
In time
You say
You've done it all
You do cool things all the damn time
And I just keep escaping from the demons
in my mind
Is life fair?
I'm in despair
Palpitating like it's the end time
Taking a deep breath trying not to lose my
mind
I am high on emotions
Every second of the day
There is some thing or the other
I'm trying to grow out from or run away
Is this how I am supposed to live?
Teach me something about life
Cause my knowledge about it is really not

working
Or am I just thinking too much?

Lovers

We are lovers
We'll get used to each other's habits
Until one of us would want to put an end to it
We'll drop the love bomb unaware of the horrors
It's gonna lead us to

Your touch, your smell, your smile
Everything is going make me fall for you
And I would gladly want you to ruin my life
Until I start cursing you for every single thing you did to me
I wonder what does love make us do?
I'll lose my mind thinking about if we're forever
And then proceed to destroy the present moment
Fearing you will never love me enough

What's "enough" though?

Will gluing myself to you would be the end of the problem?
If that happens, I will run away for my personal space

But I swear I try so hard to understand you
What goes on in your mind?
What do you think about me?
Am I everything you've ever wished for?

I know
We will tear us apart
We'll bring the death to our sanity
But anyways, we're lovers
Born to be each other's madness
We're gonna alter our brain chemistry
Wishing we'd never met each other

But hey! I love you
And I think it's too late to step back
You're mine
To love
and I'm yours
To destroy

Damaged Goods

I feel like I'm damaged goods
Surviving on the edge
I break down every single day
Wondering when will it end

Every morning so hard to pass by
I get anxious all the time
Thinking about the way I am
And how I am losing my shine

Memories and nostalgia
Keep making it all even sadder
I climb two steps up
Until something again breaks my ladder

I'm on the ground
Panicking
Overwhelming thoughts
Make me sick

Somebody tell me
It's gonna be all right

Somebody tell me
I will win this fight

I can't-
I can't-
I can't-
No more
I'm scared all the time
That I'm going to fall
Again and over
Down the hill
I miss those days when I ruled the peak

I'll be all right
I'll be all right
It's just a bad day
It's just a bad day
I'll be fine

What A Time!

I was just doing fine
Until I thought of making you mine
What a time!
Oh, What a time!
Last august was a beautiful ride
Oh, what a time!

I had my best days
My best laughs
And even one of my best birthdays
All of it with you
Everything felt brand new
Oh, what a time!

I loved you like
I had never loved anyone before
Your laughter in the hall
And the way you used to say "Yesh!"
Slept like a baby
In my arms
Where you'd rest

But it all faded into memory
Ended in time
When in September
We said our last goodbye

Oh, what a time!
Last august was a beautiful ride
Back then
I had my best life
Oh, what a time!

You Want Me I Want You

Hormones rushing through our bodies
And then the feelings start to kick in

You say
You want me
I say
I want you
We both know where it could lead

I'm so starved for your love
You're so starved for my touch
We're so starved for each other
Put your body on me

I'm gonna make you feel so much better
This is the heaven
That could heal
Our broken tortured souls
Deprived of love
We're not alone

I've been feeling like

I'm on cloud nine
I don't know
If you'd ever leave
But all I know is
This moment is so pure
I'm truly grateful for
All that we have achieved

“Light Of My Life”

"Light of my life"
You said jokingly
About saving my name
On your calling screen

I've been wanting to meet you
Making plans
Ruining my schedule
I just wanna be with you

Past Midnight

Past Midnight
I'm sitting in my room
Trying hard to sleep
I can't simply do

Tired of this feeling of
What future holds for me
I know I'll be fine
But it feels so scary

How long would the struggle stay?
Sometimes I just want to run away
Run away to a new place
Where there's always smile on my face

It's past midnight
I'm sitting in my room
Listening to my demons
About the next thing I'm gonna screw

How long do I need to be stressed out?
Sometimes the voices get too loud

Can I get a break from it?
The overthinking
That my mind cooks is just pure shit

I try every day
I hype up myself
I sit with my sadness
When my serotonin's not up
I hit my low
Dive deep into the blue
I pick myself up
Then I feel all good

But it's the mid-night
Past the witching hour
When I'm still struggling to sleep
What has happened to me?

I just keep sitting in my room
Trying hard to sleep
Which I just can't simply do

Oh My! Oh My! Oh My!

I've been doubting my beliefs and my morals
I've been laying low for the past few months
Scared to love
What if my heart breaks again
Anxious much
Like I'm gonna puke

But then you hold me
And made me calm
Understood me like no one else did
Assured me and told me
You would be here
When I'm tough to love
Or acting insane

You make me blush
In the sweetest way
You give me peace
Every single day
Even if I tell myself

Not to fall for you soon
You make me break
My own goddamn rules

Just so I could be with you

Oh my! oh my! Oh my!
You're so good to be true
Oh my! oh my! Oh my!
And I'm glad I met you

I've been building walls around me
My whole entire life
I've been not letting anybody in
Cause it is just the way I like

But then you stepped in
And my walls came down
Your magic so strong
I feel good when you're around

You feel like home
Comfortable and safe
And when I see your face

It leaves me amazed

Even if I tell myself
Not to fall for you soon
You make me break
My own goddamn rules

Just so I could be with you

Oh my! oh my! Oh my!
You're so good to be true
Oh my! oh my! Oh my!
And I'm glad I met you

For A Very Long Time

I met you in a cafe on the winter solstice
Your smile so inviting I fell all in
I couldn't get my eyes off of your pretty face
I loved holding your hands as you made me feel safe

I just wanna say to you
I would like to get to know you so much more
There seems to be a great potential
That I could be your forever
And you could be my lover
For a very long time
Or maybe for the rest of my life
I get so lost in your voice
Make me yours
I wanna make you mine

On the way home
I kept thinking about you
If I ever had to

I'd fight for you

Waited for your call
Waited for your text
Waited for you every day
I was impressed

Those four cocktails
That you made me try
I had the time of my life
With you that night

I just wanna say to you
I would like to get to know you so much
more
There seems to be a great potential
That I could be your forever
And you could be my lover
For a very long time
Or maybe for the rest of my life
I get so lost in your voice
Make me yours
I wanna make you mine

Yeah for a very long time
Or maybe for the rest of my life
I get so lost in your voice
Make me yours
I wanna make you mine

My Money

I hope you quickly return
My money on time
Cause I really can't then wait
To completely throw you out of my life

Hello/Goodbye

I blush at the mere thought of you
This feeling is something brand new
I'm noticing every little detail
I have my eyes on you

I'm ready to give my all to you
With you my heart just blooms
I go crazy when you touch me so right
I dream of you every single night

Things just fall into place
When I have you by my side
But there's a blurry line
Between your love and ignorance
Which feels so off sometimes

Is everything you've made me feel
Built on a lie?
I can't seem to understand you
No matter how much I try

But I know the end

In the back of my mind
How all the exciting hellos
Will turn into the most tragic goodbyes

You're So Beautiful

You're so beautiful and it hurts me
That you're not mine
The hope in your eyes is endless
And the sparkle in your smile is something
I live for
Why don't you talk to me more?
Why don't you have time for me?
I want to know your story
I want to be with you
Be with you in your arms
While I look into your eyes and kiss you
My plan is to make you fall for me harder
But whom should I blame the failure on?
The distance or the time?
I keep thinking about you
Like I have nothing in my life but you
It's true
I hope it could be me and you

The Conversation

And there is nothing more
You have to talk on the call
Then tell me how the fuck
Am I supposed to move
The conversation on?

The dry "Ohs" and the "Yeahs"
Do you really got nothing to share?
Oh god you're boring me to death
The beginning itself is driving us to the end

How can I save it alone?
You're not even trying

The Waiting

I kept checking my phone
Like an idiot
Wishing to have received
Something from you
And every day
You let me down

I kept drowning in
The waiting
That never ended

How long could hope have kept us alive?

Is There More?

Lately I have been feeling that
The hunger
To want more
Has died inside me

The bore seems to be creeping in
Am I not exciting anymore?
Was it all I ever destined to be?
Or is there more to my story?

The Very Last Time

Your ignorance, my naivety
Your uncertain phases, my unsettling impatience
What were we meant to be?
And what have we become?

Do you remember
The last day of the summer
When we were together for
The very last time?
The sweet silly end to the evening
When you were chasing me in the balcony
And I was just running away
Giggling screaming out of laughter
You were the hunter
And I was pure chaos

I swear I never knew
We wouldn't be 'us' after that
Were we ever 'us' in your mind though?
I think
I was too much for you for the moment

Maybe you were still restricted by your past trauma
You channelled it on me my being avoidant

I keep thinking about your aura
Your energy
Which you said was "dark"
It took me months to realise
How accurate you were

I am the brightness
You were the black hole

I don't know if you ever missed me
If you ever were sad because we ended
I wish you could've asked me to stay
Just one time
And I would've been your forever

But no,
You were never meant for me
And time showed me the truth
Now I'm so glad I'm not yours
Because you never belonged to me

Versions of Myself

All the versions of myself cannot coexist
At the same time together
So I have to let my past self be free
In the memory lane
Not caged in the jail of nostalgia

Exit Signs

Every time it's the same
You love I run
It's new
I don't know what to do
Every day I feel like
I'm going insane
Chasing the exit signs

Oh god! Tell me how to love
When there's someone
Who's doing it all right to me
I fear
I am going to ruin every thing
In the name of it is what it is

I fall down from the sky
Living for the high
But there's nothing in me to glow
When I feel all low

So tell me what can I do?
To make myself understand

I keep making same mistakes
My growth never stands a chance

I've learned enough times
But I'm still at the same point
It's like something is holding me tight
Which is why I always disappoint

Exit signs
They're like the curses in my life
Exit signs
Please let me stay sometimes
Exit signs
I'm tired of them all the time
Exit signs
I'm gonna make what's mine

Black & White

I think
You're the pessimism to my optimism
Dullness to my shine
Sadness to my happiness
You're the darkness to my light

Make It Through?

My brain's going haywire
I don't know what to do?
Is it me? Am I the problem?
Will we make it through?

Perfectly Fine

Why am I becoming someone who I am
not?
These days I get overwhelmed by every
single thought
My anxiety levels are all time high
I run from the hellos fearing the goodbyes

Where did all my life lessons go?
I cannot handle this new low
Feels like I'm losing myself again
My biggest enemy is my own fucking brain

Spoiler alert
I know how it's gonna end
I'll grow out of this sadness
And one day I won't have to pretend

I don't know when I'm going to be
perfectly fine
Well, till then I'll let my happiness wait for
me in the line
In the meantime, I'll handle myself with

care
And teach myself
Be in the moment cause that is what it's all
there

Can I Call You 'Babe'?

You sent me a picture of you today
And when I looked at it
My heart goes
Hey! Can I call you "Babe"?
For the rest of my days
I wanna spend the nights
Holding on to you so tight
I'd never let you go
Please don't say no

You said you had an alter ego
To which I replied
I like both of them
Your wicked smirk
And your sweet smile
Two characters of a person
I so want to make mine

Cause when I see you
My heart goes
Hey! Can I call you "Babe"?
For the rest of my days

I wanna spend the nights
Holding on to you so tight
I'd never let you go
Please don't say no

I'm delicately holding my emotions
I'm scared you might not love me back
But it's okay
Take your time
To reflect on us and realise
If you feel the same or not
If you wanna stay or be gone?
I've been thinking about you
Since the day we've met

Cause you made my heart go

Hey! Can I call you "Babe"?
For the rest of my days
I wanna spend the nights
Holding on to you so tight
I'd never let you go
Please don't say no

Now We Don't Talk Anymore

Now we don't talk anymore
And isn't it for the best?
We didn't turn out what we thought we could be
Oh god! I feel so light in my chest

I broke down, hit my low
When I ended it on the call
Stopped eating, cried a lot
I wandered through the empty halls

Called my friends to vent it out
But nothing really helped me really
I had to throw you out of my mind
Cause my health was starting to get ugly

You weren't good for me
I wasn't good for you
We might had it all in the starting
Cause it was all so good to be true

Until we ruined everything
We destroyed it all
Now I don't know you
And for you too I'm just gone

How Long?

How long will I keep fearing
The mistakes I did in the past?
How long will I stop myself from
Loving someone else
Just because of the heartbreak
You made me go through?
How long am I going to take
To get over you?
How long is this 'how long?'?
An eternity?
A fucking lifetime?
A moment?
How long?

You Said

You said we could make it work
If we had pure intentions
You said I could talk to you
If I start to panic
You had an ocean to give
You said you would stay
Then why did you make me wait
Till the very last day?
Why did you keep me stranded?
I kept begging for your time
But then your sweet words were whispered
That made me forget all your crimes

Your charm so magnetic
Your face of an angel
We never stood a chance
Cause you always felt like a danger
To my peace
To my sanity
To everything I was hoping we could be

Life's so much better now

Since we have called us off
I breathe the fresh air now
Couldn't have survived in all the pretending
I should've listened to my gut feeling

Story Of the Past

Something that started a year ago
Is now just a story of the past
Poured myself all into you
For us to be until the last
Hope became my poison
That started killing me fast
But you never tried to save us, darling
The magic we had has passed

There seems to be no next
We weren't built to last forever
The love we had was short lived
All our "Always" turned into "Never"

Words And Actions

How long could I have lived
Suffering in the doubts?
Your words called me in every time
But your actions threw me out

Good News

I have good news
I have a big smile
I have moved on
It's all in the past

I am over it
I laugh about it
I just don't care
It did not last

Gave you my everything
You just deserve nothing
Poured myself onto you
How long could I have drained myself?

You would do the same
If you were me
Love can really make you go crazy

I threw myself into the hell fire
I wish I knew how to save myself
I died screaming in suffocation

Heavy chest with blurry vision

Silence seemed to be the only way
To find myself lost in this intense pain
But the attachment made me scared of it to my death

Can someone teach me how to live again?

I forgot everything I knew
Somewhere lost in the heartbreak blues

I'm sad
I feel frozen every moment
I pity myself every single day
When will this end?
I can't survive this anxiety
What if I die tonight?
Will then I find peace?

The Progress

These days I feel better
I feel better in every way
It was just a bad time
Bad time giving me bad days

Slowly but gradually
I started picking myself up
Restless days
Sleepless nights
Got through the horrors
I survived
Now I find myself
Growing up
Growing out
Learning things
I'm doing all fine

Cause these days I feel better
All the damn time

Forget You

I think
I don't have to forget you
I don't think I can
But I have outgrown you
In every way
You were not made for me
And I was just lost in denial
All the love's dead now
You're now a closed chapter of my past

What Went Wrong?

You can see a smile on my face
It's a lie
How did I end up here again?
I'm surprised

Was hoping I would fall in love with you
Cause everything I felt for you was true
Until nothing was right
Not cool
You didn't see my cry for help
What can I do?

Tell me baby, what went wrong?
Was my love too much for us to get along?
You said you had phases like 'these'
Where you'd left me wondering just for
your own ease
Sucking all my hope
Dimming all my light
It was getting dark
So I had to say goodbye

Goodbye
It was fun when you were with me
Goodbye
Now I hope you'd be happy
Without me
Goodbye
For teaching me so many things
Goodbye
For whatever we couldn't be

Losing It All

Everybody's settled
Everybody's sorted
Everybody seems to be
Living their best lives

I'm still stuck
In the chaos of my past
Figuring out a way
So fucking desperately

I'm trying to catchup
But I really can't
I'm trying to run
But my feet won't work

Put me out of my misery
I'm tired of the sympathy
I'm losing it all
I'm fucking losing it all!

Starved

I gave you my everything
Until one day
You decided not to acknowledge me
anymore
Maybe I was overfeeding someone
Who wasn't even hungry
Or maybe you kept me starved from day
one

"It Wasn't That Deep"

I think I think too much
About everything that's happening
I get stuck in a thought spiral
Until I lose my mind

I think I over-analyse
The shit you said to me
Jokingly you'll laugh at me saying
"It wasn't that deep"

But it hurt my feelings
And you're still laughing
It isn't cool
It isn't right
You have ignored me every time
I've told you not to say it
But you still say it
Out loud
I feel invisible
small
I feel like you don't care about me at all

Ocean Drops

You said you have an ocean to give
Then why are making me beg for drops?

"I'm Going to Leave"

There was an ache in your voice
When I said
"I'm going to leave"
Cause you couldn't see
But I knew where it would lead

Look Through Your Eyes

Sometimes I wonder
How you'd look at my pictures now?
But then I realised that
It's not my job to see
My life from your eyes anymore
It never was my job anyway

Best Of Luck

Your shitty room
With the broken bed
Your empty soul
And the vibe so dead

Romanticised everything we had
You stink of boredom
Had to run away, I'm glad

How long could I have watered the plant
Who always wanted to die?
How long could I have drained myself
When all you wanted was to hide?

I'll be alright, babe
I'll be fine as fuck!
Try your darkness on someone else
I wish you best of luck

A Guide To A Happy Life

Is there something I'm not doing right?
Is there some guide to living a happy life?
I've tried all the ways to eliminate this pain
But all my hard work is just going into the
vain

Moving On

I started dreaming about you too soon
Thinking of you
I was over the moon
Call me a fool, obsessed, naive
Now all the love is dead and I can't revive it

Got so tired of begging for your time
Go do all your work, babe
You've been putting me on hold for
months
But now I've got no patience for you or
yours ways

I've been moving on
I am so done
Angry, irritated
But trust me, the whole situation has been
so fun

Hard work pays off
Hard work earns
Hard work is the key to success

Hard work returns

Wish you best of luck
For you and your world
Fuck it I'm out of that
Go give your ocean to some other person

Just Like I Still Am

I am falling apart again
Days are so hard to pass by
Nights are even worse
I'm trying to distract myself
With everything I can
But I'm just failing in everything
I'm just losing my mind
I feel this is going to last forever
I feel stuck
Will someone come and save me this time?

I don't think so
I guess, I have to rise above all the lies that
My mind keeps telling me
The voices drag me down to hell
I feel so fucking stupid

I keep catastrophising my thoughts
I feel like I'm going to die
But I know I am going to shine bright again
Just like I used to be
Just like I still am

You're Not in My Life

Who knows I'm posting fake smiles
Every day the aesthetics hide
My pain, my misery
I'm at the lowest
Can somebody see it?
I'm not feeling the greatest
I reach out to my friends
With tears in my eyes
They listen to my stories
And tell me I'm gonna be alright
I wake up everyday
Just to hear my head say
'You're not in my life'
Yeah, you're gone from my life
What do I do?
Where do I go?
I'm just not fine at all
What went wrong?
How did we end up here?
I could've stayed forever
If you would've asked me to
But now you're just

Lost and gone
Well… I'm so glad
You're not in my life anymore

All The People

To all the people
I liked once
To all the people
I did leave

It was magic
What we had
It was tragic
What we couldn't be

To all the people
Who broke my heart
To all the people
I was mean

We were meant to be
For a short time
We had to set each other
Free

I couldn't be more grateful
I couldn't thank enough

For all the experiences
That we shared together

Now I hope you find someone
Who'd never bring you in the situation we were in

We were never born to be together
I'm so thankful for all the lessons we taught each other

Born To Say Goodbye

I had to remind myself
Who the fuck was I
Because the day it all ended
I felt like I was going to die
Held myself so delicately
But now I stand tall and high
I guess it wasn't anyone's fault
We were just born to say goodbye

Everybody Makes Mistakes

Break the patterns
Create a new way
Don't let anything
Ruin your day

You've come so far
Fighting every day
Moving from the pain
You're gonna be okay

Give it some time
You need a little break
To sort out your shit
Cause everybody makes mistakes

Nothing

Now when I think about you
Nothing comes to my mind
The memory of being loved by you
Is not special anymore
You're just an ordinary person to me
Everything you've made me feel
I've outgrown it

I laugh about the heartbreak I went through
It's all cool now
I'm more than fine

I loved all the kisses and the cuddles we had
I liked all the time we spent together
I read all the poetries I wrote about you
Well... I'm proud of my art
But they're all funny to me now

And if I'm being honest
I think I'm going to burn them all
Can I tell you the truth?
I've had actually burned them all

Last October itself

It feels so good to finally
Feel like myself again
You're nothing to me
And maybe that's what
We were meant to be
Nothing!

Happy

I have been talking about my emotions
With my therapist
And she told me
It's healthy what I have been doing
My feelings are valid
And it's okay if
I am going to take some time
To get over the short love we had

I am allowed to feel sad
Grieve about it

Trust me I'm doing good
And I have had no hate for you
Since day one
It's the hope of what we could have been
That haunts be sometimes

Maybe in some other universe
We are together
And if this is how we are meant to be
I'm happy

Dear Summer

Dear Summer,

It's so good that you're back again
I missed your warmth immensely
I have so much to tell you
But firstly, I want to adore you
I want to soak up the sunshine
I wanna get lost in the silence of the noon
The colours of the evening
And the life that blooms
I want to dance to my summer playlist
All the fucking time
I want to drive around screaming
How much I love this life
The golden hour and that
Feeling of being free
The sky so colourful
Dear Summer,
You have everything I need
The darkest days are gone
And so is my pain
Dear summer,

I want you to stay forever
Please don't ever leave me again

A Brand-New Life

I'm shining bright high again
Leaving all the darkness in my past
Carrying the hope within myself
Creating magic every single day

I am who I am
Whatever the moment defines
Not a single second ahead
Not a single behind
I feel good in my own vibe
I am so grateful to experience
The surprises of the life

I adore the sun
I live the night
I talk to the moon
I am made up of light

Nothing ever can take me back
No one can push me into the void
I am optimistic, kind and a little bit of fun
Moving towards a brand-new life

Acknowledgments

Covers (both front and back) by my dearest friend, Anjali Dixit. Really thankful for all those fun brainstorming sessions we had. Loved the final output so much! I'm obsessed.

Some design help for the covers was also obtained from Vecteezy (https://www.vecteezy.com/)

A big shoutout to my family, my friends and my cousins who have always been supportive and have been there for me. Getting over this heartbreak wouldn't have been possible without you all. I love you all so much!

Last but not the least, a special thanks to my therapist. I will forever be grateful for all the things she taught me. Life felt lighter and easier after those sessions.

Thank you, universe, for everything :)

www.ingramcontent.com/pod-product-compliance
Lightning Source LLC
LaVergne TN
LVHW041129150826
845673LV00007B/2244

* 9 7 9 8 8 9 5 5 6 6 6 8 8 *